Made in United States
Troutdale, OR
12/10/2024

26240756R00061